THE BOY
FROM BOWRAL

For Sam Arch and all young cricketers

This edition published in Australia in 2008 by
Walker Books Australia Pty Ltd
Locked Bag 22, Newtown NSW 2042, Australia
www.walkerbooks.com.au

Originally created and produced by
Palazzo Editions Ltd
2 Wood Street
Bath, BA1 2JG

www.palazzoeditions.com

Designer: Robert Walster
Consultant: Jim Kerr

10 9 8 7 6 5 4 3 2 1

The National Library of Australia Cataloguing-in-
Publication Entry:

Ingpen, Robert, 1936- .
The boy from Bowral : the story of Donald Bradman.

1st ed.
ISBN 9781921150647 (hbk.).

1. Bradman, Donald, Sir, 1908-2001.
2. Cricket players - Australia - Biography. I. Title.

796.358092

Printed and bound in Malaysia by Imago

The BOY from BOWRAL

The story of Sir Donald Bradman
by Robert Ingpen

WALKER BOOKS
AND SUBSIDIARIES

LONDON • BOSTON • SYDNEY • AUCKLAND

Bradman's mother Emily was born in Bowral.

Bowral

Don Bradman as a choirboy in Bowral, aged about nine.

4

Don Bradman's father George was the son of an English migrant attracted to New South Wales by the gold strikes in the 1850s.

Bradman's older brother, Victor.

Bradman's sister Lilian taught him to play the piano and later became a professional music teacher.

Bowral Boyhood

One hundred years ago, in 1908, the Wright brothers were still learning to fly the world's first aircraft. The children's classic *The Wind in the Willows* was about to be published; a Melbourne schoolboy, J. A. Prout, scored 459 runs for Wesley College, and on 27 August Donald Bradman was born in Cootamundra, New South Wales. His father George Bradman was the son of an English migrant who came to seek gold near Bathurst, New South Wales. His mother was a

Whatman – a family of many keen cricketers in the Bowral District, south of Sydney.

The Bradmans lived on a farm near Yeo Yeo in the Riverina, and before Don was three they moved to live in Bowral. His father bought a weatherboard house and took a job as a carpenter. Don's older brother Victor and older sisters Islet, Lilian and May went to Bowral Primary School.

Boyhood for Don was very much the same as that for any small-town

boy of that time before the First World War. Bowral was a classic Australian country town – a self-contained community close to the road and railway that connected Sydney with Melbourne. There were two newspapers, four hotels, two banks, a gasworks, a hospital, primary and secondary schools, and the Bowral Cricket Ground. The youngster grew up in a cricket-loving community, and heard the game being discussed regularly by his family.

5

Don's uncles, George and Richard Whatman, were keen cricketers and encouraged him in the game. He began school when he was five, but there was little organised cricket or coaching. All he could do was watch the games of schoolyard cricket played by bigger boys. They fashioned their bats from handily shaped tree limbs. Their ball was a despised 'compo' – a solid orb of cork. Their wicket was chalked on the base of the school's bell post. What they knew of the game they had learned from books or folklore, or imitated from the Saturday matches played by grown-ups in Glebe Park or the Bowral Cricket Ground.

The high-school boys started to invite Don to join their games occasionally, but he found it difficult to get much practice. His parents would not allow him to roam away from home in search of fellow cricketers, so he ended up inventing games in which he was his own opponent.

The schoolyard of Bowral Primary School, in which Bradman played his earliest games. The wickets were chalked on the base of the school's bell post.

7

Using the laundry door as a wicket, Bradman
threw a golf ball at the tank stand. The
curved, uneven brick surface made it rebound
at constantly varying angles at high speed.

Don played tennis by hitting a ball against the garage door, and football by kicking a ball around in the yard behind his home. Then he began to play cricket using a stump and a golf ball. A rainwater tank, set on a round brick stand, stood near the back veranda. This covered a concrete area that became a cricket pitch for the famous Bradman game. A laundry from the house completed a covered area, open on one side, in which he could play in all weather.

Constant practice made the young cricketer skilled at his solitary game. He had to move with great speed and accuracy: holding the stump in his left hand, throwing the ball with his right, and then switching the stump to both hands in time to hit the ball as it bounced back to him. Sometimes he pretended he was left-handed and used the stump just with his left hand.

Bradman dressed for
work as a real-estate
clerk in 1924.

The young Bradman in 1926,
when his exploits in the Berrima
District cricket competition
brought him to the attention
of the NSW state selectors.

Alf Stephens, batting on his own back-yard cricket pitch, which was often used by Bradman. Stephens was a Bowral businessman and official of the cricket club who did much to encourage the young cricketer.

This lonely activity showed its benefits in his schoolyard game, because the older boys were impressed enough to invite the 11-year-old to join a more formal match. It was played on a rough piece of ground alongside the main Bowral Oval in Glebe Park. The captain of Don's team won the toss and went in to bat. The first two players were dismissed for ducks and Don faced a fiery fast bowler. He played his first ball in 'grown-up' cricket with the skill he would demonstrate thousands of times during the next 30 years, and beside a ground that would one day be named after him. The bowler's chance of a hat-trick was foiled and the young batsman carried his bat for 55 runs.

People in Bowral began to take a more serious interest in his self-taught cricketing skills, and his Uncle George, who played for the Bowral team in the Berrima District, invited him to be scorer for the 1920–21 season. One Saturday the team travelled to Moss Vale but found themselves short of an eleventh man, and they agreed to give young Don a game. Batting at eighth wicket, and wielding a full-size bat, the 12-year-old scored 37 not out in the first innings and 29 not out the next Saturday at first wicket down.

As a reward for his debut performance the team gave him a cricket bat. It was old and battered, but it had a real splice. Don's father sawed three inches off the bottom and rounded it off. Later that season Don made his first 100. Playing for his own school on matting, the young right-hander startled onlookers with a dazzling 115 not out, out of a total of 156.

That year he also made a two-day trip to Sydney with his father, and this fired his enthusiasm for the game. They watched play in the fifth Test between Australia and England. Don never forgot the remarkable innings by Charlie Macartney of 170 on the great Sydney Cricket Ground. On the train back to Bowral he told his father, 'I shall never be satisfied until I can play on that ground'.

The Modest Hero

234 n.o.

The Bowral Oval in Glebe Park It was on this pitch that Bradman first encountered the bowler Bill O'Reilly in December 1925, and broke the Berrima District record with his score of 234 not out.

Don left Bowral High School at the end of 1922 after passing his Intermediate Certificate, and began working for a real-estate agent in Bowral. For a time he even abandoned cricket to play tennis. He did not put on cricket pads for Bowral again until 1925–26 – the season that was to begin the legend of 'The Boy from Bowral'.

That year was one of the most important in his whole cricketing career. Aged 17 he was now a regular member of the Bowral team. In one game against Wingello he made 234 not out in less than three hours! He had some luck along the way by being dropped twice in slips off the bowling of a promising leg-spin bowler called Bill O'Reilly.

Don followed this with a score of 300, spread over three Saturdays against Moss Vale. His season – which yielded 1,318 runs at an average of 94-14 over 13 innings, and not out nine times – did not go unnoticed in Sydney, where first-class cricket was played. On 5 October 1926 he received a letter from the New South Wales Cricket Association, inviting him to 'attend practice' at the Sydney Cricket Ground on the following Monday at 4 p.m. The letter, in part, read as follows:

Don Bradman at the crease during his early years playing cricket in Sydney, where he represented St George.

D. Bradman, Esq.,
C/o A. Stephens, Esq., Booley Street, Bowral
Dear Sir:

The state selectors have under consideration your record in cricket in the past season, and in view of such record they particularly desire to see you in action. For this purpose I would like you to attend practice at the Sydney Cricket Ground on Monday next, 11th instant. Practice commences at 4 p.m. and continues through the afternoon. Should you be able to attend as requested, please let me know in order that I may inform the selectors who will be on watch for you and in order that I may advise you as to further particulars. My Association is prepared to pay your fare from Bowral and return; should you deem it necessary to remain in Sydney overnight you will be reimbursed to the extent of your accommodation...

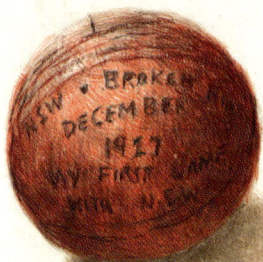

The cricket ball used in Bradman's first match for NSW at Broken Hill in December 1927.

Bradman faced Clarrie Grimmett for the first time in Adelaide in December 1927. Bradman made 118 in his debut first-class innings, but Grimmett took 8 for 57 to help his team beat NSW by one wicket.

The selectors were looking mainly for bowlers for the State team to play Queensland in the Sheffield Shield. They watched 40 young bowlers and batsmen demonstrate their skills in the nets on the Sydney Cricket Ground. One of the many journalists there that day wrote for his Sydney newspaper: 'Great interest was shown in the knock of the Bowral wonder, Don Bradman… He was quite undismayed by the size of the gallery, and has undoubted talent. On the short side, he uses a short-handled bat, but makes powerful strokes around the wicket.'

Don's life started to become busy. He had to rise early each Saturday to catch a train to Sydney so he could play for St George. He rarely got home until midnight. During the week his job in the real-estate agency demanded careful attention, and then he had cricket practice on hard wickets. He still found time for tennis and a new interest he shared with his older brother Victor – motoring.

In 1927, playing again for Bowral, Bradman broke his own local record, with a score of 320 not out, including six sixes and 43 fours. In December that year he was selected to join the State Sheffield Shield team to play the southern states. In Adelaide, cricket lovers had heard something of 'The Bowral Wonder' and watched keenly to see how he would cope with the wily spin of Clarrie Grimmett, their own State hero. They were impressed when Don, batting No. 7, hit him for two fours in the first over. He eventually made 118 – making him the twentieth Australian to score a century on his first-class debut.

Don Bradman batting during his historic
innings against Queensland in January
1930 on the Sydney Cricket Ground.

452 n.o.

Don Bradman made the Australian Test team for the first game in the Ashes series in Brisbane in 1928. He scored only 18 in his first innings and one in the second, and was dropped for the second Test. In the third Test in Melbourne he made 79 and 112 for his first Test century. In Adelaide he made 40 and 58, and finally in Melbourne for the fifth Test, 123 and 37 .

His confidence grew with this amazing run-making, and in the next season, 1929–30, he created a world record of 452 not out in a phenomenal 424 minutes for New South Wales on the Sydney Cricket Ground against Queensland. A newspaper reported the innings:

'Sydney Jan 7. Alan Kippax declared and stopped the slaughter as Don Bradman might have made 500 or even 600 against Queensland. He was certainly well settled in when Alan Kippax declared the NSW innings closed at 8/761. Bradman was 452 not out, and the Queenslanders had the sporting grace to chair him off the field, smiling broadly and definitely looking fit enough to carry on. But they were so undone by the onslaught that they capitulated in their final innings for 84, leaving NSW the winners by 685. Bradman reached 100 in just 104 minutes, 200 in 185 minutes, 300 in 288 minutes and 400 in 377 minutes, and passed Ponsford's previous record as he went on to his score in 424 minutes.'

Another paper that day commented: 'Today he can with safety pack his bag and label it: D. Bradman, Australian XI, England.' Needless to say, Don was a member of Bill Woodfull's team that left Fremantle on the Orient liner *Orford* in early March 1930.

After his record-breaking 452 not out, Queensland cricketers 'chair' Don Bradman off the SCG.

Impact on England

On 30 April Don had his first experience of an English county cricket match. The Worcester ground was typically English – surrounded by great elm trees, with the peal of Worcester Cathedral chimes marking the hours. The weather was like a fine midwinter day in Australia, with the sun briefly showing and a cold wind blowing.

Worcester batted first for a modest 131 runs, and at last it was Bradman's time to play his first innings in England. The conditions could hardly have been more different from the matting and concrete wickets of Bowral or the true turf of the Sydney Oval. The lush, soft Worcester surface seemed dotted with little piles of dirt – worm casts – that left the turf slippery and uneven. In partnership with his captain Bill Woodfull – who had experience of English conditions – Don followed his technique for the first 115 minutes and completed his first century on English soil. Woodfull's wicket fell when he reached 133, but Bradman continued scoring remorselessly. Men in the stands would later boast that they had been there to see young Bradman knock up his first century in England. During his innings of 280 minutes he made 236 first-class runs.

With this, Bradman began a string of innings that had a massive impact on England. He went on immediately against Leicestershire to make 185 not out in even worse conditions, then 78 not out against Yorkshire. By the end of May, one month after his first innings in England, he had scored 1,000 runs. He was the only Australian to achieve this feat – and the actual Ashes Tests had not even begun…

The Worcester Cricket Ground, with Don Bradman batting during his first appearance in England in 1930. He scored a double century, the first of three such scores on the same ground.

Bill Woodfull captained
Australia between 1930
and 1934.

Bradman in action with the
great English wicket-keeper
George Duckworth, who caught
him out to end his historic
innings of 334 in the third
Test at Leeds in 1930.

The London Evening News on 17 June 1930 had no doubts about the most important batsman in the Australian team.

Reporting on the fifth Test at the Oval, the London Star on 20 August did not need to mention who 'he' was when Duckworth caught Bradman off Harold Larwood for 232.

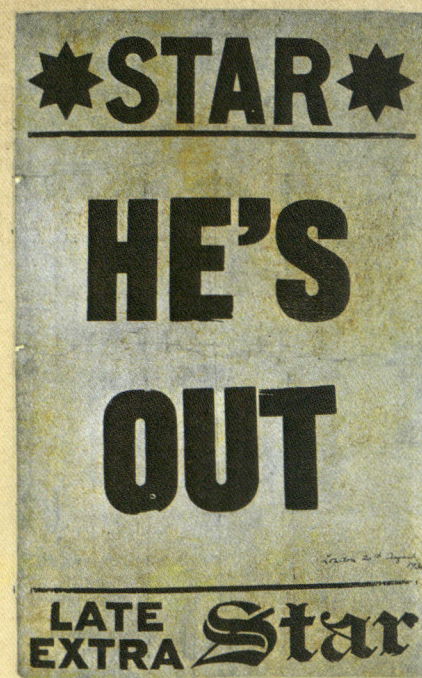

BRADMAN v. ENGLAND

JUNE 17, 1930

EVENING 6.30 NEWS

★STAR★

HE'S OUT

LATE EXTRA *Star*

By the time the Australian team arrived at Trent Bridge, Nottingham for the first Test, beginning on 13 June, they were quietly confident, but English cricket lovers did not really know what to make of the visitors. They had won or drawn all their first-class games, but their performance had been erratic.

English sportswriters predicted that England would win. One of them wrote: 'England is not only the favourite, but a hot one. Supposing the Australians were Englishmen, then only Bradman and Grimmett would be chosen for England.'

England batted first and made a modest 270, but Australia lagged well behind, with only 144 in the first innings, Don making only eight. In the second innings he was much more watchful of the accurate bowling attack and made 131, but Australia lost the game by 93 runs.

In late June the Australians took on England at Lords for the second Test. Bradman was strangely missing before the game and did not join the teams to be introduced to the Duke of York (later King George VI). There was consternation among the Australians – until Don eventually

turned up after the toss, just before the first ball was bowled. He claimed he had 'merely slept in'.

England again batted first, and made 425. Then, at first wicket down, Don treated the crowd to a huge innings – 254 runs out of a total of 729 for the loss of six wickets. Much later he recalled that this was technically the most perfect innings he ever played. Don Bradman remains the youngest batsman to score a double century in a Test for Australia, and his batting time of 245 minutes for reaching 200 set a Test record in England.

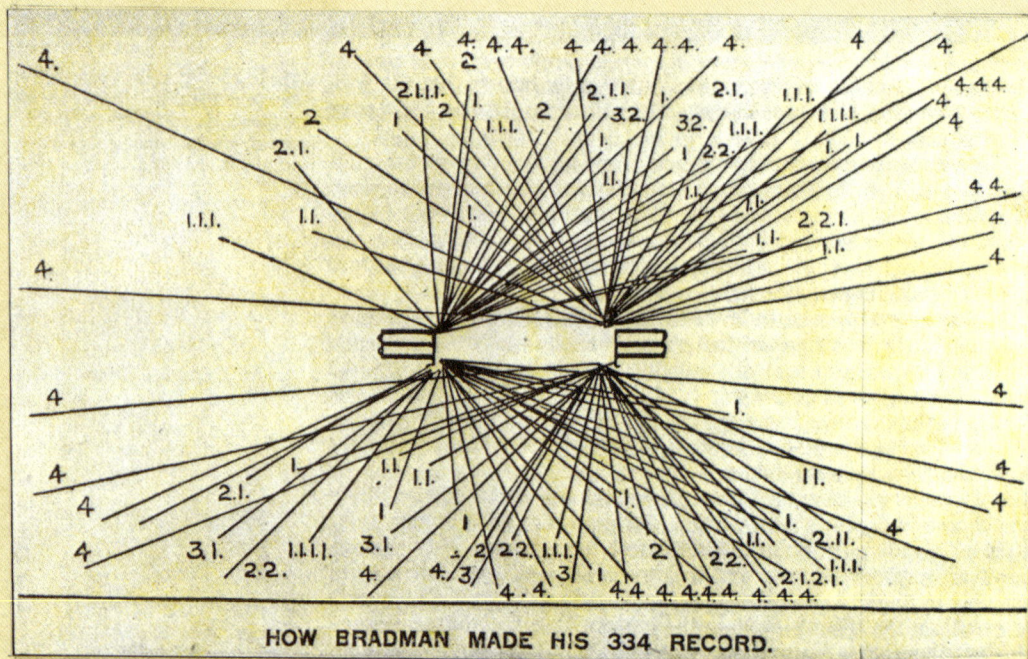

HOW BRADMAN MADE HIS 334 RECORD.

This chart appeared in an Australian newspaper to illustrate the scoring strokes of 46 fours, six threes, 26 twos and 80 singles, which comprised Bradman's historic 334 at Leeds.

The third Test at Headingley in Leeds saw Australia batting first. Don scored 100 before lunch. By tea he was at 220, and after five hours and 36 minutes he reached 300. Off the last ball of the day an off-drive brought his score to 309, and his total runs for the tour to 2,000. The next morning Don added another 25 to his score before he snicked a ball from Maurice Tate to the English wicket-keeper George Duckworth. The English press shouted with relief in a poster that announced simply 'He's Out!' The 21-year-old had made 334 runs.

He could have been chaired through the streets of Leeds if he had chosen to expose himself to publicity after that astonishing batting performance. Instead, he stayed in his hotel room to listen to music and write letters home. Of that the press observed: 'Don Bradman is the most elusive man of all – a more level-headed young man or one less likely to become spoiled by admiration never wore flannels.'

By August, in the fifth Test at the Oval, the Ashes was emphatically won with another invincible batting display by the Australians. Needless to say, Don was at the forefront, with 232 runs, his wicket finally taken by English fast bowler Harold Larwood. Within a year or two Larwood would feature in probably the greatest controversy ever in the Ashes.

The Australian tour of England concluded with Bradman having batted seven innings of 974 runs in the Tests, at an average of nearly 140. This score was far ahead of any other player – on either side. Clarrie Grimmett was nearly as far ahead in the bowling, with 29 wickets in five games.

334

The English cricketers applaud
and Don Bradman raises his bat
to acknowledge the crowd after
he completes his third century in
one day at Leeds.

Don arrived back in Australia to a hero's welcome and a tiring round of off-field publicity. The first series of Test matches between Australia and the West Indies was scheduled to be played in Australia between December 1930 and March 1931. It seemed that the strain of a prolonged tour and other off-field problems were affecting the hero's cricket. In Adelaide for the first Test he went in at 55 runs for one on the second day, playing 15 minutes for only four runs. Even so, two days after that – and on the same Adelaide ground – he made 258 for NSW in 282 minutes, helping his team to a victory over South Australia by an innings and 134 runs.

In Sydney, for the second Test against the 'Windies', he made only 25, while Bill Ponsford top-scored with 183. The home team won by an innings and 172 runs. In the third Test in Brisbane, Don more than made up for his performances so far. He reached 200 in just over four hours, and finished the day with 223 not out. This score broke Victor Trumper's 1910–11 record for an Australian at home in a Test match.

In the fourth Test, Don made another fast 100 in front of enthralled spectators at the Melbourne Cricket Ground. In making 152, he made his century in even time. However, in the fifth Test – which the West Indies won by 30 runs – he made 43 in the first innings and then the first duck in his Test career. He was bowled by pace bowler Herman Griffith, who had easily the best tour bowling figures for the West Indies.

Herman Griffith, the West Indies bowler who dismissed Bradman for his first duck in Test cricket.

The South African tour of Australia in the 1931–32 season was the first for 21 years. Don's scores before they arrived in the State games produced more ducks. The first came when he was dismissed by Aboriginal cricketer Eddie Gilbert. One of Gilbert's rocket-like deliveries for Queensland smashed the bat clean out of Bradman's grasp. Later he wrote: 'I unhesitatingly class his short fast burst as faster than anything seen from Larwood or anyone else.'

Don overcame his minor slump with some magnificent batting against the South Africans. He played in six matches against them –

four Tests and two games for NSW – and scored three centuries and three double centuries. In the fourth Test, at Adelaide in January, he carried his bat for 299. Don had then caught his boot sprigs in the coil matting of the dressing room and badly twisted his ankle, and as a result he did not bat in the fifth Test.

Don Bradman married his long-time friend Jessie Menzies in April 1932. His brother Victor was best man and Jessie's sisters were the bridesmaids. They were married in Sydney and drove to Melbourne for their honeymoon. The most glamorous part of this holiday turned out to be a carefully planned trip with an Australian touring team to the United States and Canada. It was an unofficial tour organised by Don's close friend, Arthur Mailey.

When they arrived in New York the newspapers compared Bradman with Babe Ruth, the great baseball champion of the 1920s. Arrangements were made for the two sportsmen to meet and watch a baseball game between the New York Yankees and the Chicago White Sox.

When Don and Jessie returned to Sydney they looked forward to having time to settle into their first home together. In fact it became a refuge from the outside world, where everyone seemed to want attention from their idol.

Don began the memorable 1932–33 season playing for his old club St George, scoring an effortless century in 64 minutes. Meanwhile the English team, under the captaincy of Douglas Jardine, had already embarked for Australia aboard the liner *Orontes*.

Jessie Menzies

Jessie Menzies married Don Bradman in Sydney on 30 April 1932. Jessie had grown up in the farming community of Glenquarry, some way from Bowral, and her parents knew the Bradmans well. There was no school bus in 1921 when Jessie first went to the Bowral Primary School. The distance was too far for a little girl to travel each day by herself, so the Bradmans offered to let her stay with them during the week and return home at the weekends.

Jessie was a pretty, lively girl, about a year younger than the Bradman's youngest child, Don. She settled easily into the Bradman home and lived there until she and her two sisters could safely travel each day from home by horse and buggy. Jessie and Don were occasional playmates.

After Bowral High School, Jessie went to business college in Sydney and then on to work with the Commonwealth Bank. She lived with her sisters in the suburb of Burwood, not far from where Don Bradman boarded when he made his move to Sydney in 1926.

Bradman's unconventional batting grip: 'Some noticed this freakish grip and advised a change. Bradman would not hear of it. It had served him well and would, he believed, continue to do so.'

The Run-maker

One of the many newspaper reports of Don Bradman on Australia's unofficial tour of North America called him 'The World's Greatest Player', and went on to say: 'Don Bradman, Australia's Babe Ruth of cricket, did his stuff with the bat and ball for the edification of Vancouver fandom yesterday afternoon.' For a non-cricketing but sports-loving North America, it was interesting to listen to onlookers' remarks about Bradman's run-making skills:

'I don't know where he gets all that power.'

'He must have a powerful pair of wrists and his timing must be perfect.'

'Just look how he stands. His footwork is about perfect and he seems to always be in position to hit any kind of ball.'

At the same time, in New York, a journalist wrote of the meeting that had taken place between Babe Ruth and Don Bradman:

'The Babe was surprised by Bradman's lack of size and weight. Don weighs 145 pounds, is 24 years of age and according to cricket experts … is a scientist rather than a powerhouse. Bradman hits them where they ain't. Babe remarked to Bradman "From what they are telling me I thought you were a husky guy. But us little fellows can hit 'em harder than the big ones."'

In a biography of Don Bradman published at his retirement in 1948, cricketer A. G. Moyes wrote about Don's exceptional qualities and the peculiarities that he thought helped make him the greatest of batsmen. Moyes acknowledged Don's quick eye and speedy footwork, and drew attention to the peculiarity of his grip on the cricket bat. He wrote:

'With most players, the handle runs across the palm of the hand and rests against the ball of the thumb. With Bradman, the hand is turned over so far that the handle presses against the ball of the thumb. As the grip tightens, the pressure becomes more intense. The left hand is turned so that the wrist is behind the handle. This means that whether he is attacking or defending, danger to the fingers and back of the hand from a ball that lifts unexpectedly is reduced to a minimum. The combined result is that the bat slopes at an angle of forty-five degrees from the ground, and so keeps the ball down, ensuring that in both the hook and the cut, the blade is automatically turned over the ball. Some noticed this freakish grip and advised a change. Bradman would not hear of it. It had served him well and would, he believed, continue to do so.'

The following page of drawings illustrates Don's batsmanship. The drawings are made with the help of photographs taken in London in 1930, which were reproduced with the cricketer's notes in *Don Bradman's Book*.

The stance at the
wicket, awaiting the
bowler's delivery.

Off drive

Hook shot

Forward defence

Square cut off the
back foot

Back defence

Bodyline!

Larwood's orthodox field placing, 1928-29.

In October 1932 the English cricketers arrived in Perth for an Ashes tour of 17 first-class matches. There were rumours that their captain, Douglas Jardine, had a plan to combat the run-making of Don Bradman following his grand performance against them in 1930.

Jardine's anti-Bradman plan was based firstly on 'leg-theory' – that is, the idea that balls pitched on the leg stump with a field weighted on the leg side are difficult to score from. The plan was also based on an observation by British speed bowler Harold Larwood, who said: 'Don didn't like the balls rising on his body. He kept drawing away.'

By November a word had been coined to describe this tactic – 'bodyline'. A well-respected newspaper columnist, and ex-football and cricket legend, Jack Worrall, described the bowling by Larwood and Bill Voce as 'half-pitched slingers on the body line'. The name immediately caught on.

Later on, after this infamous series between Australia and England, the Australian Cricket Board of Control adopted a more lengthy definition of bodyline: 'Any ball delivered which, in the opinion of the umpire at the bowler's end, is bowled at the batsman with the intent to intimidate or injure him, shall be considered unfair, and "no-ball" shall be called and the bowler notified of the reason.' At the time, though, there were no written rules against this controversial tactic by the English team.

After a couple of uneventful matches Jardine unveiled his secret weapon against the Australian batsmen Bill Woodfull, Don Bradman and Stan McCabe. On 30 December Don Bradman walked slowly on to the MCG to the sustained roar of the greatest sporting crowd in the world. First ball, he faced Bill Bowes. He

expected a fast 'bodyline' bouncer and got into position to hook. It was short, it was slow, and Bradman edged it on to his stumps. Australia eventually won the game by 111 runs, which was close to the 103 runs Bradman made for Australia in the second innings.

The bodyline tactics of the England captain in the third Test at Adelaide brought relations between Australia and England to crisis point. It began with Larwood's last ball of his second over to Australian captain, Woodfull. This delivery jumped up from a short length outside the off stump and fizzed back at Woodfull, who had expected it to fly harmlessly by. It struck him above the heart, he staggered and dropped the bat, but he was quick to recover, and continued his innings. Larwood immediately aggravated the already angry atmosphere both on and off the pitch by altering his orthodox field to a 'bodyline' one for his third

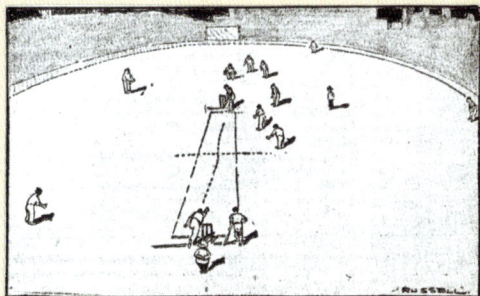

Larwood's 'bodyline' field placing, 1932–33.

The manager and captain of the 1932–33 England team, P. F. 'Plum' Warner, later Sir Pelham Warner, is on the left. Douglas Jardine (right) was described as 'best-hated man in Australia' during the bodyline series.

In the second Test at the Melbourne Cricket Ground in 1932–33, Bradman batted before a crowd of 63,993 people. He was out first ball to fast bowler Bowes of England. It was the only Test wicket Bowes took during the tour.

and following overs. All hell broke
loose – with anger aimed mostly at the
England captain Jardine.

After play that day the England team
manager, P. F. 'Plum' Warner, offered
Woodfull his sympathy and an apology
for the on-field behaviour of his
cricketers. In response Woodfull made his
famous statement: 'There are two teams
out there on the oval. One is playing
cricket, the other is not.' The Cricket
Board of Control formally contacted the
Marylebone Cricket Club in London,
saying that bodyline bowling was
detrimental to the interests of the
game and several angry telegrams were
exchanged. The Australians were furious
at the bodyline tactic, and the English
were outraged at the suggestion they were
behaving in an unsportsmanlike manner.
For a time it looked as though the series
might be called off altogether, but
eventually an uneasy truce was reached.

England won the Test in Adelaide
by 338 runs, although no big scores
were made by either side. In Brisbane,
England won again by six wickets
and then by eight wickets in the final
Sydney Test. And England took
controversy and the Ashes back home.

Harold Larwood – the English
fast bowler on whom the bodyline
tactics depended. He took 64
of his 78 Test wickets against
Australia. In all first-class
matches he took 1,427 wickets
at just 17.21 runs per wicket.

Larwood bowls to Bradman in the Sydney Test. Bodyline depended on field placements. Batsmen were left unable to defend themselves without the near-certainty of edging a catch to the cluster of close-in leg-side fieldsmen.

Don Bradman moved to a new career and cricketing life in South Australia in March 1934. He was 25 years old and employed by the stockbroker firm of H. W. Hodgetts in Adelaide.

In his final game for NSW he scored 128. His other Sheffield Shield scores included 200 against Queensland, then 187 against Victoria. In the domestic season of 1933–34 he topped everything with 1,192 runs in 11 innings for an average of 132.44.

The Ashes tour of England in 1934 began with Bradman making another double century of 206 against Worcestershire. But even his team-mates started to get worried as his usual flow of runs began to dry up. In his first three Tests he scored only 133 runs in five innings. In the fourth Test at Headingley, however, he more than made up for his run of outs by treating the Yorkshire crowd to 304 runs to match his 334 in 1930. Don had to weather some hostile bowling at the start, and at three wickets down the Australian score was only 39. Bill Bowes had just got Bert Oldfield and Bill Woodfull for ducks.

There was a hush over the ground as Don faced the first ball, and a great roar as he drove it through mid-on for four. With Bill Ponsford (181), Don moved the score to 427 and Australia was safe. The pair did it again in the fifth Test, with a second wicket partnership of 451 – at that time a record stand for any wicket in Test cricket. Don's 244 took 316 minutes.

In September, still in London, Don fell ill and had an emergency operation to remove his appendix. He suffered complications after the surgery and news of his illness covered the front pages of newspapers in both England and Australia. Even the king asked for regular bulletins on Don's progress, and the aviator Sir Charles Kingsford Smith offered to fly Jessie Bradman to London so she could be with her husband (in fact she ended up going by boat). Don's condition began to improve, and he slowly recovered – but his cricketing future looked in doubt.

Bill O'Reilly produced his greatest spell of bowling in the first Test at Nottingham in 1934. He took 11 for 129, defeating England almost single-handedly.

Bradman and Bill Ponsford at the Oval in 1934. They made 451 runs in 316 minutes — at that time, the highest stand for any wicket in Test cricket. In total Ponsford made 266 and Bradman 244.

451 partnership

Captain of Australia

Don did not play again until November 1935. He made a quiet 15 and 50 for South Australia against an England MCC XI on its way to New Zealand. But then it was as though he suddenly came to life. He made 117 against NSW, 233 against Queensland, then 357 against Victoria. He then topped the lot with 369 against Tasmania. This score beat Clem Hill's old record of 365 for South Australia.

Don Bradman was appointed Australian captain for the first Test in Brisbane against England in the 1936–37 season. Douglas Jardine had been replaced as England's captain by George 'Gubby' Allen, who had refused to use the dangerous bodyline tactic in the 1932–33 series. Bradman and Allen knew and respected each other, and they both looked forward to their first meeting as captains. This was scheduled for 29 October, when

South Australia played the MCC at Adelaide. However, Don awaited another event with more excitement. Jessie gave birth to a son on 28 October. Sadly, though, the sickly newborn died on the day the match opened. The groundsmen lowered the Adelaide oval flags to half-mast out of respect, and Don did not play.

The weather played a big part in helping England win the first two Tests in Brisbane and Sydney, but it then assisted Australia in the third and fifth Tests in Melbourne.

The third Test opened on New Year's Day in 1937 at the MCG. Don won the toss for the first time as captain, and Australia batted. Bad weather threatened and he declared Australia at 200 for nine, forcing England to bat on a 'gluepot' wicket that he later described as 'the worst I ever saw in my life'. When the English captain realised what Don's strategy

would be, he declared for 76 runs, and Australia was forced to spend the rest of the day on the gluepot wicket. And all this was happening in front of 65,235 spectators.

Don put in his bowlers – O'Reilly, Ward and Fleetwood Smith – as night-watchmen while the wicket dried. The following day, a mammoth crowd of 87,798 turned up to watch Jack Fingleton make 136 and Don 270. Australia won by 365 runs.

There was no rain in Adelaide, where Australia levelled the series – helped by another Bradman double century (212) and 10 wickets by Fleetwood-Smith. A reporter summed up the decider Test in Melbourne: 'A mere 169 from Bradman, and another "special" from Stan McCabe. Then the rain came and spiced up the pitch for O'Reilly.' Australia won easily by an innings and 200 runs, and the Ashes returned to Australia.

By May 1938 the Australians were back in England for another Ashes tour – this time with many new faces. Don Bradman surpassed himself by scoring 1,000 runs in only seven innings. He started out with his usual double century of 258 at Worcester. He then scored 137 against Cambridge and 278 against the MCC. On the eve of the first Test at Trent Bridge his tour average was 170.15.

In England's first innings of the first Test, three centuries and a double century were made in a total of 658 for the loss of eight wickets. Australia replied with 411 and 427 for the loss of six wickets, helped by 232 from Stan McCabe in the first innings and 144 not out by Bradman in the second. The match was drawn. Don was so impressed by McCabe's innings that he called to his team-mates, 'Come and watch this. You'll never see anything like it again.'

The second Test at Lords was also drawn, with Bradman making 102 not out in the second innings and

Walter Hammond making 240 for England in the first. At Leeds – where Australia won – Don was again top scorer, with 103 runs.

But now it was England's turn. At the Oval for the final Test, Len Hutton made 364 runs in a long and dour innings. This surpassed Bradman's Test record of 334 and helped England to a total of nine declared for 903, and a win by an innings and 579 runs. In that game Don bowled 2.2 overs, but retired after fracturing his ankle when he stumbled in an O'Reilly footmark while bowling leg-breaks.

Back in Australia for the domestic season of 1938–39, Don had recovered from his broken ankle. Here he reminded fans of his batting brilliance by making six centuries in

six innings in six matches. As he had made centuries in the last two innings before the 1938 tour of England, he had scored eight consecutive centuries in Australia – a record that has still not been broken.

The winter of 1939 brought a welcome relief from cricket. It also brought the Bradmans great joy, as their son John was born on 10 July. Two months later the Second World War began, and Australia found itself drawn into the conflict. Most of the world became involved in the war and many international sporting events were curtailed. Like most Australians of military age, Bradman enlisted, hoping to join the RAAF.

In the 1939–40 season, Don remained head and shoulders above the rest, scoring 1,475 runs at 122.91, including 251 not out as well as 90 not out in South Australia's win against premiers NSW. He went on to score 138 against Queensland, 267 against Victoria and 209 not out against Western Australia.

After the War

In June 1940, Bradman joined the Royal Australian Air Force, hoping to be a pilot or at least air crew. During a medical examination to determine his fitness for such service, it was found that the 'eagle eyes' of the great batsman were beginning to falter and his general health was below the standard required. He transferred to the army as a lieutenant and was based at Frankston, Victoria in the Army School of Physical Training before he was due to embark overseas. His health began to suffer and he spent time in hospital about the time his second child, Shirley, arrived in April 1941. By June an army medical board had invalided him out of the service, and after a long period of recovery in Mittagong, NSW, he returned with Jessie and their two children to Adelaide to work as a stockbroker.

In the 1945–46 season, after a break of many seasons of cricket and several bouts of bad health, including a leg injury, Don finally played again for South Australia. He started with a 'painstaking' 68 and 52 not out against Queensland, and 112 against an Australian Services XI captained by Lindsay Hassett. But Don had other problems. The stockbroking firm he worked for in Adelaide had collapsed, so he eventually set up his own business on the Adelaide stock exchange.

Australia gave a hero's welcome to the first post-war Test team from England, led by Don's old rival Walter Hammond. After the tune-up games against the State sides, the England team arrived in Brisbane feeling confident that they would beat the less experienced Australians. Bradman won the toss and batted. He made 187 of the Australian total of 645. England made only 141 in their first innings, and had just commenced their 'follow-on' when a tremendous rainstorm turned the Brisbane Cricket Ground (the 'Gabba') into a lake. When play eventually resumed they were bundled out for 172.

Just before Christmas 1946, playing in Sydney, Australia chased England's modest 255. Bradman, batting down the list because of a leg injury, joined Sid Barnes at the fall of the fourth wicket, with the score on 159. Six and a half hours later Don was out for 234, and four balls later Barnes joined him – out on 234. Australia won by an innings and 33 runs.

The next two Tests, in Melbourne and Adelaide, were drawn. During the Adelaide Test on Don's home ground, Jessie and the six-year-old John had to leave the match early so they could beat the crowd. As they were leaving they heard a huge roar. John said, 'That'll be Dad'. And it was. Bradman bowled Alec Bedser 0. The final Test of the 1946–47 season resulted in Australia keeping the Ashes.

A party of 17 Indian cricketers arrived in Australia to play 14 matches, including five Tests, in October 1947. Although India had first toured England in 1932, they had not visited Australia before.

Before the tour the Indians had expressed a sportsmanlike wish that Don Bradman would score his hundredth first-class hundred against them. In November they got their wish. He made 172 in this, only his 295th innings – a feat approached by no other batsman.

The first Test in Brisbane was marred by rain, and Australia won easily. Bradman was the top scorer, with 185. Despite this, the crowd felt that he had let the Australian innings go on too long and he lost some popularity. Rain meant that only two hours play had been possible on three of the six days, and play had been abandoned altogether on day five. In that time India managed only 58 and 98.

The Sydney Test was drawn – only 10 hours of play had been possible because of rain. In Melbourne for the next Test Bradman made 132 out of a total of 394, and India did better with 291 and 125. Australia won by 233 runs.

In Adelaide, Bradman made 201 with Hassett and 198 not out to carry Australia's first innings to 674. India totalled 381 and 277, to lose by an innings and 16 runs. For the final Test at the MCG, Australia easily won again, with the young Neil Harvey making 153.

In the entire series Australia had to bat twice in only one of the five Tests. Bradman, the 'old man' who was now fondly referred to as 'The Don', did well – 185, 13, 132, 127 not out, 201 and 57 retired hurt.

Don Bradman returns to the pavilion after his dismissal in the third Test at the MCG in January 1947 against England.

The Don and the King. Don Bradman with King George VI in Scotland between games. Bradman was criticised by some for having his hands in his pockets in the presence of royalty!

The Invincibles

Don Bradman was nearly 40 years old when he led the Australians back to England in 1948 for the first tour after the war. The spearhead bowler for the side was Ray Lindwall, following his success against England in Australia the previous year. Keith Miller was feared as a shock opening bowler as well as an exciting batsman. Only four of the 17 men in the touring party had been to England previously – Bradman, Hassett, Barnes and Brown.

At Worcester, Don refrained from scoring the double century he had achieved on his three previous visits, settling for 107. Before the first Test at Trent Bridge on 10 June, the Australians had won six and drawn two against the county sides. Against Essex they scored four centuries in one day's batting for 721 – a world record.

The first Test was practically over on the first day, when England made only 165. The Australian innings lasted well into the third day. They made 509, Bradman scoring 138 and Hassett 137. England then made 441, leaving Australia only 98 to get. They did this easily, even though Bradman was again bowled by Bedser for a duck. Australia won the Test at Lords and drew at Old Trafford.

The England team should perhaps have won the fourth Test at Headingley. Australia scored an astonishing 404 for three wickets in less than a day. Arthur Morris made 182 and Bradman was on 173 not out at the finish. They had to rewrite the record books to win – becoming the first team to score more than 400 runs in a final innings to secure victory.

At the Oval on 18 August, a few days before his fortieth birthday, Don Bradman walked to the wicket for the last time in Test matches. The applause from the capacity crowd rose to a crescendo as the English captain, Norman Yardley, called for three cheers and shook his hand. Don seemed quite moved by the reception and took some time to compose himself before he settled over his bat to face leg-spinner Eric Hollies. He had to make four runs to average 100 in his entire Test cricket career. He played the first ball and the next was a wrong 'un on a perfect length – Bradman went forward and was bowled off an inside edge. A mighty roar went up.

The rest of the match was an anticlimax – England had made 52 in its first innings and was staring at defeat, with Australia at two wickets down for 153 at stumps. The next day Arthur Morris went on to make 196 and Australia completed an invincible series with a win in the final Test by an innings and 149 runs.

Don played a number of farewell games in Australia in 1948–49. In Adelaide he made a few runs in a testimonial game for Arthur Richardson. The most publicised was his own testimonial at the Melbourne Cricket Ground. It was a light-hearted affair that took place before 94,035 cricket fans across two days. He made 123, but many years later

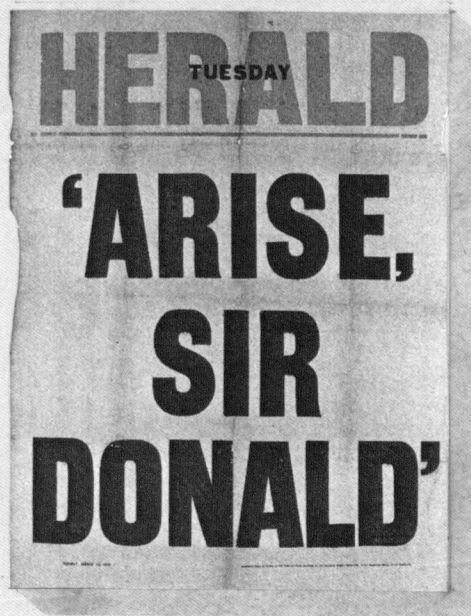

HERALD TUESDAY
'ARISE, SIR DONALD'

he indicated in a letter to Michael Page and myself that he did not include this among his 18 first-class centuries on the MCG.

On 15 March 1949 Donald Bradman was knighted for his services to cricket by the governor-general Sir William McKell. He came to Canberra with Jessie for the ceremony. After the investiture he chatted with the governor, who was an ardent cricket follower and had his own stories of watching the great Victor Trumper in club cricket in Sydney, about the time Sir Don was a schoolboy from Bowral.

Bowral Today

In 1976 the people of Bowral gave the name of Bradman Oval to their old sports ground in Glebe Park. Alongside was to be the Sir Donald Bradman Museum. The guests at the ceremony included Sir Donald and Lady Bradman, and former team-mates including Bill O'Reilly. The Oval is exactly the same site where the two men had faced each other some 50 years earlier. To the amusement of the guests, Don took block on the pitch and Bill O'Reilly, then aged 72, sent down a delivery outside the leg stump. Don tried to hook it and missed. That was his last appearance on a cricket pitch. Don died on 25 February 2001 after a bout of pneumonia. He was 92.

Final Scoreboard

Donald George Bradman
Born: 27 August 1908
Died: 25 February 2001
Right-hand batsman

First-class debut: 1927–28
234 matches, 28,067 runs
69 50s, 117 centuries, average 95.14

Test debut: 1928–29
52 matches, 6,996 runs
13 50s, 29 centuries, average 99.94
32 catches and two wickets

SCORES IN AUSTRALIA (FIRST CLASS)

Year	Innings	Not Out	Highest Score	Runs	Average	Centuries
1927–28	10	1	134	416	46.22	2
1928–29	24	6	340 n/o	1,690	93.88	7
1929–30	16	2	452 n/o	1,596	113.28	5
1930–31	18	–	258	1,422	79.00	5
1931–32	13	1	299 n/o	1,403	116.91	7
1932–33	21	2	235	1,171	61.63	3
1933–34	11	2	253	1,192	132.44	5
1934–35	Did not play					
1935–36	9	–	360	1,173	130.33	4
1936–37	19	1	270	1,552	86.22	6
1937–38	18	2	246	1,437	85.81	7
1938–39	7	1	225	819	153.16	6
1939–40	15	3	267	1,475	122.91	5
1940–41	4	–	12	18	4.50	–
1941–45	Did not play					
1945–46	3	1	112	232	116.00	1
1946–47	14	1	234	1,032	79.38	4
1947–48	12	2	201	1,296	129.60	8
1948–49	4	–	123	218	54.00	1

SCORES IN ENGLAND (FIRST CLASS)

Year	Innings	Not Out	Highest Score	Runs	Average	Centuries
1930	36	6	334	2,560	98.50	10
1934	27	3	304	2,020	84.16	7
1938	26	5	278	2,429	115.66	13
1948	31	4	187	2,428	89.92	11
Total	**338**	**43**	**452 n/o**	**28,067**	**95.14**	**117**

TEST CRICKET

	Innings	Not Out	Highest Score	Runs	Average	Centuries
England	63	7	334	5,028	80.78	19
West Indies	6	–	223	447	74.50	2
South Africa	5	1	299 n/o	806	201.50	4
India	6	2	201	715	178.75	4
Total	**80**	**10**	**334**	**6,996**	**99.94**	**29**

Who is the Best Ever?

During the second Test against England in 1946–47, umpire Jack Scott said that Donald Bradman was a better batsman than Victor Trumper – regarded as the greatest Australian batsman prior to Bradman – and Scott's opinion carried a good deal of weight. In 1907, as an 18-year-old, he captured the wickets of Trumper and Monty Noble in his initial game in Sydney first-grade cricket. Scott became the best-known of Australia's Test umpires from 1936 to 1947, after playing as a fast bowler for New South Wales and South Australia. He never played Test cricket.

Scott made his comments about Bradman during a discussion of the second Test in Sydney, where Bradman had made 234 runs. He said: 'I never thought I would see anyone better than Trumper or Macartney but Bradman is the greatest batsman Australia has ever produced. Some of Trumper's strokes were more brilliant but with Bradman you never know what he is going to do.'

Bradman remains far ahead in run-making. His 234 in Sydney made him the only batsman to score double centuries in Test matches at Sydney, Melbourne and Adelaide, and on both grounds at Brisbane. His Test average of 97.14 for the 1946–47 season remains a record, and the next year against India he became the only Australian to make 100 first-class centuries.

Trumper opened his first-class career in the 1894–95 season at 17, and played his last match in 1914, his career spanning 20 years. In his 380 completed innings he made 42 centuries. In Tests he played 89 innings for 3,163 runs at an average of 39.04.

By comparison, Bradman's first-class career ran from 1928, when he was 19, to 1949. From this period we have to deduct four years during the Second World War when no first-class cricket was played. Bradman's career was three years shorter than Trumper's. In his 295 completed innings he made 117 centuries at a ratio of 39.6 per cent (Trumper's was 11.05 per cent). In Tests he played 80 innings for 6,996 runs at an average of 99.94.

These statistics show that there is no comparison between the two men, especially when considering the advantages Trumper enjoyed under the rules of his own era. For example, during Trumper's time the ball had to be between 23 and 23.5 cm in circumference, while during Bradman's career it had to be between 22 and 22.5 cm. This reduction in size must have been an advantage to bowlers, since the smaller ball would have been more difficult to hit. Today the ball size is between 22.4 and 22.9 cm.

During Trumper's time, batsmen had to defend stumps 68.5 cm high and 20.3 cm wide, whereas during Bradman's career the wicket area was larger by 14 per cent – 71.2 by 22.8 cm. There are also bat sizes and technology, differing LBW (leg before wicket) laws and pitch conditions to be compared.

Victor Trumper, Test cricket debut, 1899.

45

Throughout the whole of Trumper's career, the LBW rule stated that the ball needed to pitch in a line between wicket and wicket for a batsman to be given out LBW. In 1937, the LBW rule was changed so that a batsman could be given out to any ball that hit the legs while pitching outside the off stump. Bradman therefore had to contend with this extra rule for the last half of his career.

This didn't seem to worry him, for in 1938, under the new law that favoured the bowler, he averaged

Don Bradman, Test cricket debut, 1928-29.

Ricky Ponting, Test cricket debut, 1995–96.

61.9 in 21 completed innings. In 1902, Trumper averaged 20.75 in 53 completed innings.

Bradman was also a master of different pitch conditions. For example, he averaged 64.7 on rain-affected wickets – which are much more difficult to bat on – in England. This compares with Trumper's career average, on both wet and dry pitches, of 44.5.

A good way to compare batsmen is to calculate the number of completed innings a batsman played for each century scored. In doing this we can see that Bradman's figures are more than twice as good as any other player who has ever lived. He scored an average of 39.6 centuries for every 100 completed innings. Next to him is Walter Hammond of England with 18.6 per 100. Trumper appears well down the list – despite the advantages for batsmen in his time – with 10.5 per 100.

The present-day leading batsman and Australian captain, Ricky Ponting, has completed 345 innings to February 2007, and has made 66 centuries. His Test debut was in 1995 when he was 21. In tests he has played 183 innings for 9,368 runs at an average of 59.26. All this took place in only 12 years of first-class cricket, and with the help of generally good wickets, safety helmets, and modern cricket bats that seem to hit the ball further than was possible in Bradman's day. Ricky Ponting may one day come close to being favourably compared with the great Don Bradman.

Further reading

The following books should provide more details and statistics about the life and times of Don Bradman.

Don Bradman's Cricket Book by Donald Bradman (Hutchinson, London, 1930)

Bradman by A. G. Moyes (Angus & Robertson, Sydney, 1948)

Bradman the Great by B. J. Wakley (Nicholas Kay, London, 1959)

Sir Donald Bradman by Anthony Davis (Cassell, London, 1960)

Sir Donald Bradman by Irving Rosewater (B. T. Batsford Ltd, London, 1978)

Bradman: The Illustrated Biography by Michael Page (Macmillan, Melbourne, 1983)

The Bradman Era by Bill O'Reilly and Jack Egan (Willow, London, 1984)

The Bradman Albums Vols. 1 and 2 (Rigby Publishers, Adelaide, 1987)

Bradman, An Australian Hero by Charles Williams (Little, Brown, London, 1996)

Wisden on Bradman by Graham Wright (Hardie Grant, Melbourne, 1998)

200 Seasons of Australian Cricket (Pan Macmillan, Sydney, 1997)

Our Don Bradman by Philip Deriman (ABC Books, Sydney, 2001)

Acknowledgements

In 1982 Michael Page researched and wrote *Bradman – The Illustrated Biography* for publication as a 'birthday biography' to mark Sir Donald Bradman's 75th birthday. The book was based on Michael Page's interviews with Sir Don and on his lifetime collection of personal material. With my thanks to Michael Page for his approval, I have drawn on his work to make this book for children – *The Boy from Bowral* – which celebrates the centenary of the birth of 'The Don' in August 2008.

In depicting such an extraordinary life and career as that of Donald Bradman, I have had the good fortune of being able to review many press photographs of the great man in action. The photos that I have used as points of reference are invariably not credited to any specific source. Every effort has been made to trace the copyright holders of such photographs which have sometimes provided the basis for me to convey accuracy and reality. While providing inspiration for this book the illustrated interpretation of people, places and events is my own.

Index